ISHOP TUDOR

WHAT EVERY KINGDOM NEEDS

ISBN 9781492200321

Contents

Introduction

Since its creation, the world has been ruled by the rise and fall of kingdoms. Some of these kingdoms established governmental systems that have lasted centuries; even today, our world still has the remnants of these systems.

History records men like Alfred the Great, King of Wessex, who so improved his kingdom's legal and military systems that the British monarchy is the best known monarchy in the modern world. The current monarchy still preserves the same traditions, systems and symbolism of previous monarchs. We remember Napoleon Bonaparte—the French general, whose legal reform has been a major influence in many civil law jurisdictions worldwide today. We also cannot ignore the influence of the Kingdom of Rome which undoubtedly was one of the greatest influences on civilization and the structure of governments.

The Bible also records significant kings and kingdoms. The first form of systematic government or kingdom recorded in the Bible occurred when, Cain, the brother of Abel, *"began to **build a city** and named it after his son Enoch."* (Genesis 4:17). The word "city" in this Scripture, in the original Hebrew, means a place guarded by *waking* or a watch. This tells us that the city of Enoch had a formalized military system of ranks and watches. Then the Bible tells of Nimrod, son of Cush, who built a great kingdom, centered around the Babylonian cities of Babylon, Uruk, Akkad, and Kalneh. The Bible goes on to say, *"Nimrod then went north to Assyria and built Nineveh, Rehoboth-ir, and Calah, along with Resen, which was located between Nineveh and* **the great city of Calah**" (Genesis 10:10). The ruins of Calah today can be found in modern day Iraq, southeast Mosul. This kingdom was built so strategically with great military force and wealth that evidence of its great wealth has been found over the last 100 years; archeologists have unearthed gold, sculptures and artifacts worth millions of dollars from this ancient city. This kingdom was not broke!

The Bible gives the account of various kingdoms that have reigned in the earth, from the kingdoms of Edom to the Davidic kingdom to the kingdom of Babylon. The point is that all the aforementioned kingdoms from the Bible and records of history are powerful and dominant entities that significantly impacted society, both past and present. These kingdoms influenced how and where people lived, ate, fought, worked, prayed, and generally dictated the lifestyle of millions of people; and their imprint on modern society is clearly apparent in all of these areas today.

Why do some kingdoms last centuries and some only last a few years?

What made these kingdoms great? Why do some kingdoms last centuries and some only last a few years? How is it that the British monarchy exists today, while the Roman Empire died a slow death on the slopes of Rome thousands of years ago? What is the ingredient for a successful kingdom? Kingdoms are similar to cakes in one regard. For instance, every cake needs different ingredients to make it a great cake. If one ingredient is missing, the cake is not so great. Every kingdom, like a cake, needs special ingredients to make it great. If one ingredient is missing, the kingdom will not be successful. .

Chapter One

What Is a Kingdom?

In today's society, when we think of the word kingdom, we think of majestic castles, beautiful princesses and dashing young princes. Many of us were born in a democracy, not a kingdom, so we are naturally challenged in our understanding of kingdom structure and operations. In a world where we elect our leaders democratically, the kingdom concept is alien to us.

A kingdom reflects the characteristics of its king.

By definition a kingdom is a state or government having a king or queen as its head. A kingdom is the king's domain. It is the territory in which he has governing influence, in which his will, his purpose and intent are law and are binding. This produces a citizenry of people who express his culture and reflect his nature. A kingdom reflects the characteristics of its king.

Every kingdom has a king and that king owns everything, including the people themselves. In a kingdom, the people are called citizens or subjects. Subjects are under the domain and rule of the king and serve at the king's pleasure. Every subject has a job or purpose to fulfill, and that role is to benefit the king and kingdom as a whole.

In the introduction, I mentioned earthly kingdoms that have ruled and are ruling on earth. As human beings, we are also under the influence of spiritual kingdoms: the kingdom of darkness, ruled by Satan and his demons, and the Kingdom of Heaven, ruled by the Lord Jesus Christ. As Christians, we are subjects of the King of kings in the Kingdom of Heaven. Luke 11:2 says, *"Our Father, who art in Heaven, Hallowed be thy Name, **Thy Kingdom come,** thy will be done **on earth** as it is in Heaven."* Christ wills that His Kingdom should come to us here on earth and, ultimately, that *"**kingdoms of this world should become the Kingdom of our Lord**"* (Revelation 11:15). Christ desires that the culture of heaven should be the culture of earth.

As subjects of the Kingdom of Heaven, we have roles and responsibilities to fulfill in His kingdom. In essence we are to preach the gospel and disciple all nations. Today, Christianity is one of the largest religions in the world largely because Christians have been good subjects of His Kingdom and fulfilled His desires. However, the Bible also describes us in Revelation 1:6 as "kings" and, according to 1 Peter 2:9, *"we are a **royal** priesthood."* If you and I are kings, then it stands that we must have a kingdom; otherwise, what are we ruling? God has given us kingdoms/domains to reign over.

If you and I are kings, then we must have a kingdom

These kingdoms may be your family or your business, or your ministry. For example, as husband and father, I am king of my family. My adult boys might not agree—but I am king. My wife and children are my subjects in this kingdom; they reflect my characteristics and culture. God has given me my family as my domain. As founder and leader of Jabula, I am king over it too. God called me and placed me as the set man in this ministry. He has given me this domain. The congregants are my subjects; they reflect my characteristics and culture. As a business owner, your business is your kingdom; your employees are your subjects. They must reflect your characteristics and culture, or they will not continue to be a part of the business. It is a domain God has given you.

Many Christians are good subjects and citizens but are appalling kings. An appalling king will have an appalling kingdom. This book will teach you how to be a great king and, hence, have a great kingdom. I will explore with you twelve key ingredients that I believe every kingdom needs to be great. And as we begin talking about what every kingdom needs, remember you are a king, and you have a kingdom! Whether you believe it or not, this is a biblical fact, and the greatness of your kingdom is entirely up to you.

Lessons from Egypt

We are extracting our kingdom lessons from the Kingdom of Egypt during the time that Joseph, the son of Jacob, was second in rank in the kingdom after Pharaoh, king of Egypt. Through the lives of Pharaoh and Joseph, we learn important lessons about the functionality and protocol of kingdom living.

Genesis tells that Joseph was the eleventh of Jacob's twelve sons and Rachel's firstborn. Joseph was sold into slavery by his jealous brothers, yet rose to become the most powerful man in Egypt next to Pharaoh. By all biblical and historical accounts, this particular Pharaoh was a successful king. His nation prospered under his rule. He was successful because he surrounded himself with skilled and successful people. He had cup-bearers, chief bakers, priests, and wise men who served at his pleasure. He recognized excellence and was quick to join himself to those who were highly skilled, so he added Joseph to his team. The fact is that highly skilled people solve problems. When you have problem solvers in your team, you will grow.

In a kingdom, a king needs his subjects, and the subjects need the king

Pharaoh needed the skills and wisdom of his subjects, and his subjects needed Pharaoh's protection and covering. In a kingdom, a king needs his subjects, and the subjects need the king. That is why Jesus says, *"...without me, you can do nothing. Abide in me, and I will abide in you"* (John 15:4). When we are in Christ, and Christ is in us, our lives are extremely fruitful. Pharaoh understood this principle; so he attached himself to skilled individuals.

It is sad today to see leaders of churches and businesses fail to identify the gifts and talents in their 'subjects'. In fact some leaders abuse their subjects by exploiting their service to the organization. I have seen many promising businesses die because leaders are more concerned about what their bank statements read than about the welfare of the subjects who make them that money. World markets are in trouble today because leaders demand profit-maximization at any cost—even at the expense of employees and surrounding communities.

Pharaoh was a great king—not because he was all knowing and all powerful but simply because the sum total of the people around him made him great. I always desire to have skilled people serve with me because I know that I am only as strong as the weakest person in my team.

As a subject, Joseph also understood the impact of teams. When asked to interpret Pharaoh's dream, he spoke clearly and without fear. He presented the challenge but also proposed a solution. He knew he could add value to the kingdom and did not hide his gifting and skill. He was a team player. I have been in meetings where people hide their skills, talents and ideas in a sea of mediocrity. They are afraid to go against the flow—or to rock the boat. A 'rocked' boat eliminates the weak. The strong ones will hang on and stay with you in the boat until you get to shore. The apostle Paul was not afraid to rock the boat, when *"he withstood Peter to his face"* for his hypocritical behavior (Galatians 2:11).

We can see from Joseph's life that all the things that happened to him were training and preparation for him to serve the king. As subjects in the kingdom, we must be fully equipped. The Bible says, *"...to **equip** the saints to do the work of the Kingdom..."* (Ephesians 4:12). A subject must be equipped to fulfill his or her task and role in a kingdom setting. Far too many times, organizations and governments fail because subjects who are not fully prepared are given influential positions and roles. We see this in the life of King Rehoboam, son of King Solomon, who lost half of his kingdom because he chose to listen to the counsel of men who were not equipped in kingdom building.

When Joseph was still a young lad, he had dreams of greatness; and his father's extraordinary gift (the exquisite coat of many colors) may have confirmed his greatness in his mind. The robe of many colors that Joseph received may not mean much to us, but it was significant in that time. This multi-color robe does not mean much today because you can go into a shop and buy a multi-colored shirt for twenty dollars. However, in Joseph's day, multi-colored garments were not only expensive but they were extraordinary and prestigious; and extreme care and skill was needed to produce them. Only kings, nobles and people of stature were associated with such garments.

This extraordinary gift was just one of many factors during Joseph's youth that were symbolic of the measure of rule on his life. Joseph knew he had a big calling in life, but he couldn't articulate it or understand it. It was an abstract picture in his mind and heart. His father, Jacob, also knew that Joseph had a special calling on his life. That is why he went to a great expense to give him the robe of many colors. Jacob did not understand the facets of Joseph's calling either but the Bible says he *"kept Joseph's dreams in his mind"* (Genesis 37:11).

As Christians, we are all called to serve in the

Kingdom, but I believe we should pray specifically for a Joseph-type anointing on our lives. The Joseph anointing is the type that builds kingdoms. It is this anointing that will build ministries that touch millions. It is this anointing that will build multi-national, trans-generational companies. Joseph and Pharaoh became the most influential people in the whole world because they built a governmental structure that became a life-line to an entire region. This is a picture of the kind of influence that Christ wants us to have in the earth. For this reason, we will study the components of the kingdom of Egypt during the time of Joseph. We will look at the concepts involved in the kingdom and the key players within the kingdom and unveil the skills each of them had that added to the success of the kingdom. The following chapters of the book will discuss each key in detail in hopes of giving us a better picture of how to build a successful kingdom.

Chapter Two

Every Kingdom Needs a Dream

Proverbs 19:29 declares, *"Without **prophetic vision,** the people will perish..."* The word "vision" here in the Hebrew language is derived from the words meaning *"dream, revelation or oracle."* As leader of the most powerful kingdom on earth in its day, Pharaoh had a dream about the future of his nation. Pharaoh did not understand his dream, but the most important thing is that he dreamed. When you have a dream or vision, you have a specific direction in which you are heading. All of us should ask the following questions:

- We should ask our governments: "What is the vision for our nation?"
- We should ask our pastors: "What is the vision for the church?"
- Wives should ask their husbands, "What is the vision for our family?"

If these questions cannot be answered, then there is a huge challenge. Without vision, a kingdom will not prosper, and its people are destined for failure.

As an African, who grew up and still lives in Africa, one of our major problems is that many of our leaders cannot tell us their vision. Rather, we have Western governments and relief agencies leading and giving direction to African issues. As well-meaning and helpful as this can sometimes be, I truly believe that most of Africa's major problems will be solved when leaders begin to dream and share their dreams with their subjects. This is what Pharaoh did. He did not understand what he dreamed, but, by sharing it, he knew that one of his subjects would have the skill to interpret and bring understanding.

There is no generation that has lacked fathering like this current generation

Another area where leaders are vision-challenged is fatherhood. There is no generation that has lacked fathering like this current generation. Many children are growing up today without a father's direction. Fathers set the vision for the family—just like Joshua when he said, *"As for me and my family; we shall serve the Lord"* (Joshua 24:15). Joshua's dream for his family was clear and precise. We should be like Joshua, who set a clear-cut direction for his family to follow. Too many of our children are being guided by hip-hop music, television and the ever-growing wonder of the World Wide Web. My fear is that the next generation will be led by a people who do not fear God and give regard to His law. As fathers, we are partly to blame for our children's delinquency in this generation. In ancient Sparta, ten-year-old boys knew exactly what they would be doing in twenty years' time because they were told at a young age what their trade or profession would be. For example, soldiers began their training literally at birth, and their childhood was filled with practice, drills, and more practice. This may sound a bit extreme, but the principle behind it is not—these young children had a vision cast before them at an early age. We need to do the same for our children today; *"training them in the way they should go"* (Proverbs 22:6).

Back to Pharaoh's dream—in Genesis 41, the Bible tells us that Pharaoh dreamed of seven healthy cows being eaten by seven skinny cows and then seven healthy stalks of wheat being eaten by stricken stalks of wheat. The substance of this dream is illogical; it doesn't make sense. No wonder Pharaoh was troubled. None of Pharaoh's sorcerers and advisers could interpret the dream. Dreams that are God-inspired will often seem to not make sense. When Joseph dreamed of the sun, moon and stars bowing to him—it did not seem cogent; but when he was appointed Vizier of Egypt, and his family came to bow before him, he understood that the symbols had clearly represented his future reality.

All leaders should desire to have God-inspired dreams. These are dreams that bring global reformation. William Wilberforce dreamed and fought for the elimination of slavery. Within the fifty years following Wilberforce, most of the nations in the western hemisphere had outlawed slavery. Martin Luther King had a dream about the abolition of racial segregation and the inception of racial equality. Today, black people around the world have equal rights. The Wright brothers dreamed that man would fly—I am sure people at the time thought they had lost their minds—but today, their dream has revolutionized the way we live. I could go on and talk about the "dreamers" of history and our time, but the question is—what is your dream?

As a king, what dream has God given you? As a subject, what dream has your leader shared with you? I always share my dreams with people who are walking with us. I tell them of the 10,000-seat church we want to build. I share with them the dream of reformational businesses that are needed in Africa to eradicate systematic poverty. I continually cast the vision for my church and ministry. Some of the dreams are easy to interpret, understand and execute. Some are not easy to interpret; but the key is that I dream. My kingdom has a dream. Your kingdom needs a dream too.

.

Chapter Three

Every Kingdom Needs a Pharaoh

Every kingdom needs a leader—a king. A successful kingdom is a kingdom that has a king who lives beyond his capacity. Successful ministries, businesses and nations have leaders that have endured personal sacrifice to the benefit of their respective domains. Today, the worldview on leadership is so distorted that leaders no longer *lead*, but they *lord*. Jesus said to His disciples, *"do not lord yourselves over others but rather, the greatest in the kingdom, is he who serves others"* (Luke 22:26). A great king serves his kingdom.

A king that lords over his subjects is a dangerous and destructive king

A king that lords over his subjects is a dangerous and destructive king. This type of king enjoys the benefits and perks of power without accepting the responsibility that comes with power. When his kingdom does well, he wants all the glory and praise but when his kingdom is failing, he will find someone to blame. A kingdom with a king like this is destined for failure. No wonder many

African states today are failing. In the 16th century, when armies went out to war, the king always led them in battle. He was never at the back or the middle—always in front—leading the charge. We need our kings and leaders to be like this today—kings who are willing to die for the good of their kingdoms.

The Pharaoh in Joseph's time was one such king. When he appointed Joseph as second in command, he put his political legacy at great risk. Firstly, Joseph was a Jew, and Egyptians considered Jews an *"abomination"* (Genesis 46:34). Egyptians would not sit down to eat at the same table with Jews and also considered the profession of the Jews—who were shepherds by trade—disgraceful. The word "abomination" in its original Hebrew language is derived from the word *"disgusting."* The Egyptians considered the Jews to be a disgusting race. Apartheid and racial segregation had its roots in ancient Egypt too! However, Pharaoh did not care about this. Not only did he accept Joseph and promote him; he accepted his whole family too. I can imagine the murmurings and whisperings in the corridors and hallways of the palace. The fact is, if Joseph had failed in his tasks, the people would have blamed and accused Pharaoh for bringing in Joseph.

Secondly, Joseph did not have a formal education. The Egyptian society was an educated society, and all its leaders and nobility went through a rigid schooling program. Some of the earth's greatest inventions like the wheel, paper, and writing were invented by the early Egyptians. They were an advanced and progressive nation. Pharaoh put himself in great political risk by appointing Joseph, but he did not put his career above the interests of the nation. His personal interests and reputation came second to the interests of the kingdom.

Thirdly, the Egyptians believed in different gods, not the God that Joseph worshipped. Ancient Egyptians believed in a complex system of polytheistic gods. Their belief centered on their interaction with a multitude of deities who were thought to be present in the forces and elements of nature. The Egyptians believed these deities were in control of the elements. These gods included the sun god, Ra; the sky goddess, Nut; the creator god, Amun; and the mother goddess, Isis. The Egyptians built temples and expended tremendous amounts of resources into their beliefs. This systemized religion produced devout followers, magicians, diviners, and priests. The Egyptians were so committed in their beliefs that the Bible records that their magicians were able to replicate four of the ten plagues performed through the hand of Moses. Pharaoh himself was considered, by his people, to be a descendent of the gods. Despite Pharaoh's beliefs and the beliefs of his people, he chose Joseph. He made a kingdom decision, not a personal one.

Let us look again at what Jesus said about leadership, "*The kings of the nations exercise lordship over them.* **And they who exercise authority on them are called benefactors**" (Luke 22:25). When kings lord over their subjects, only the king and the immediate people around him will benefit. The rest of the people and the kingdom will suffer. Let's look at this practically. How many nations exist, where the leaders have amassed great wealth, while the general populace lives in poverty? How many companies do we know where the directors and CEO's are paid super bonuses while, at the same time, employees are being retrenched and taking pay cuts? How many families are there where children and wives live in fear and in the shadow of an autocratic husband and father? As a king in your domain, be sober-minded and check your leadership and motives, and your results. Are your subjects benefiting from your leadership? Is the kingdom prospering under your hand?

In the long run, the decision Pharaoh made over Joseph's role saved the kingdom of Egypt. Not only did the whole of Egypt benefit from Pharaoh's leadership, but also the nations and region around Egypt benefited too. This is the same principle we see in the Kingdom of God, where the whole of mankind has benefited and can benefit from the reign of our King of kings—Jesus Christ. The psalmist says, "*Bless Jehovah, O my soul, and* **forget not all His benefits**" (Psalm 103:2). Again he says, *"What shall I give to Jehovah **for all His benefits toward me?"*** (Psalm 116:12) We are **benefactors** in His kingdom.

In our ministry, I get great joy from seeing the congregants grow and prosper. When I see this, I know that my kingdom, given to me by God, resembles His Kingdom. I love hearing the testimonies of people, because every good report and achievement from your subjects shows that your kingdom has characteristics similar to those of the Kingdom of Heaven. The Apostle Paul wanted so much for his subjects to benefit from his leadership that he asked himself, *"Is my preaching in vain? Why do I not see you benefiting from the gospel?"* (I Corinthians 15:14). Again he says to the Philippi church, *"...I want to see that **you receive the fruit that increases to your benefit"*** (Philippians 4:17, ISV). He understood that leadership and kingship meant being a servant to your kingdom.

Chapter Four

Every Kingdom Needs an Interpreter

When Joseph stood before Pharaoh, he probably was in awe of the grandeur of the palace—the shiny marble floors, the gold door handles, and the majestic posture of Pharaoh's servants. Even the new clothes given to him were so soft and smelled of the best aromas of the known world. He had been accustomed to his prison garb that smelled of humanity and urine. Though the surroundings in which Joseph currently found himself were new to him—one thing remained constant—the Wisdom of God.

The wisdom of God is apparent in Joseph in his ability to interpret Pharaoh's dream; the response he gave as he stood before Pharaoh was God-given and ultimately saved millions of lives from starvation and death. Joseph was able to take Pharaoh's dream and present it in such a way that even laymen could understand it. Furthermore, he broke it down, gave it structure, and gave instructions on how to proceed. This is the role of an interpreter in a kingdom. He takes the vision of the kingdom and breaks it down to bite-size pieces for the other subjects to understand and to execute.

The prophet Habakkuk says this, "*Write the vision, and make it plain on the tablets that he who reads it may run*" (Habakkuk 2:2). There are three parts to this Scripture:

1.) The king is the one who writes the vision.
2.) The interpreter's role is to make the vision plain and understandable.
3.) The king's subjects are the ones that run with what is made plain and actually do the work necessary to bring the vision into reality.

The words "*make it plain*" in this Scripture, when translated literally from the Hebrew language mean "**to explain.**" The interpreter's role is to **explain** the vision of the kingdom. This role is so important because, without it, a dream remains a dream. The interpreter facilitates dreams, turning them into reality.

We see this principle in operation in Moses' leadership. Let me retell the story from Exodus. God calls Moses up Mount Sinai. While up the mountain, Moses sits in the Presence of God and listens to God. Here, God instructs Moses on His law, precepts, and commandments. God also gives Moses the blueprint to build His sanctuary, along with the Ark of Covenant and all the other things needed to make up God's Tent of Meeting. God's instructions are precise and detailed. His standard is high, and the ingredients required are of the highest quality. For example, God's instructions to make the Gold Lampstand are as follow:

> *And you shall make a lampstand of pure gold. The lampstand shall be made of beaten work; its shaft, and its branches, its cups, its knobs, and its blossoms, shall be from it. And six branches shall come out of the sides of it—three branches of the lampstand out of the one side, and three branches of the lampstand out of the other side. Three almond-like cups on the one branch, with knob and blossom; and three almond-like cups on the one branch, with knob and blossom, so for the six branches, those going out of the lampstand. And in the lampstand shall be four almond-like cups, with their knobs and their blossoms; and a knob under two branches of it, and a knob under two branches of it, and a knob under two branches of it, according to the six branches, those going out of the lampstand. Their knobs and their branches shall be of it, all of it one beaten work of pure gold. And you shall make the seven lamps of it. And one shall light the lamps of it, so that they may give light on its face. And the tongs of it, and its pans shall be of pure gold. One shall make it of a talent of pure gold, with all these vessels.* (Exodus 25:31–38)

I don't know how Moses felt, but if God asked me to make this Gold Lampstand, I wouldn't know where to start. In my mind, I know what I want. I have a clear picture of what this lampstand should look like, but I do not have the practicalities of making this picture become reality. This is where Moses needed his interpreter. His interpreter came in the form of Bezaleel, the son of Uri, the son of Hur. The Bible describes Moses' interpreter as follows:

> *And Moses said to the sons of Israel, See, Jehovah has called the son of Uri the son of Hur, by the name Bezaleel, of the tribe of Judah.* **And He has filled him with the spirit of God in wisdom, in understanding, and in knowledge, and in all kinds of work,** *and to devise designs, to work in gold, and in silver, and in bronze, and in the cutting of stones to set, and in carving of wood, to make any kind of skillful work.* **And He has put in his heart that he may teach,** *he and Aholiab the son of Ahisamach, of the tribe of Dan.* **He has filled them with wisdom of heart to work all kinds of work;** *of the smith, and of the skillful worker, and of the embroiderer, in blue, and in purple, in scarlet, and in bleached linen, and of the weaver, of those who do any work, and of those who work out artful work. And Bezaleel and Aholiab shall work with everyone wise of heart to whom Jehovah* **has given wisdom and intelligence,** *to know how to do every work of the service of the sanctuary, concerning all which Jehovah had commanded* (Exodus 35:30–35; 36:1).

From this passage of Scripture, we see some important characteristics of an interpreter:

1.) **Interpreters must be filled with the Spirit of wisdom and understanding.** Bezaleel understood how to take Moses' picture and make it reality. He had the wisdom to do so. He understood the tools that would be needed. He knew where to find the raw materials needed. He knew how much of each material would be needed. He could write the manual of how to make a gold lampstand.

Wisdom is a cornerstone to kingdom building. Proverbs describes wisdom as being present when God was creating the earth and heavens at the beginning. Wisdom describes herself saying, *"I wisdom dwell with prudence.... I am understanding, I have strength. By me, kings reign, and rulers decree justice... The Lord possessed me at the beginning of His way, before His works of old... when there were no depths I was brought forth... when He prepared the heaven, I was there..."* (Proverbs 8:12, 15, 22) When God formed the earth and heavens, wisdom was His right hand companion.

When God formed the earth and heavens, wisdom was His right hand companion

We too must have wisdom at our right hand. This wisdom is found in the interpreters that God has filled with the Spirit of Wisdom. The 21st century church greatly honors its apostles and prophets, but now we must honor the wise men in our midst. If you look closely at the kingdoms that have prospered greatly, you will find wise men and counselors around the king who have influenced the king to make the right decision.

(2) **Interpreters must be able to teach others.** Interpreters must have the ability and gift to teach others. The interpreter must take what is in the king's mind and present it to his subjects in a way that they understand. In Jesus' three-year ministry on earth, we see that He did more teaching than preaching. He was trying to get the people to understand what He saw in His Father's heart. He would teach the people what He saw in His Father's heart using simple parables and illustrations in the hope that the people would catch the Father's vision. Christ is the Father's interpreter; thus John says, "*You cannot go to God without going through Christ*" (John 14:6). God the Father is revealed through Christ the Son. Likewise a king's dream is revealed through his interpreter.

In today's world, these interpreters are given titles like: General Manager, Chief of Staff, Deacons. Regardless of the title we give them, these men and women are important to kingdom building. For dreams to become reality, we need interpreters.

Chapter Five

Every Kingdom Needs a Baker

Several years before Joseph stood before Pharaoh, Joseph got to meet his baker in prison. For the baker, it would be a short-lived relationship, as he was executed by Pharaoh's men a few days later. However, in the time he was in prison with Joseph, he described how he baked bread for Pharaoh. I am sure he described to Joseph some of his favorite bread recipes.

Across all social classes, bread was central to the diet of ancient Egyptians. Bread was consumed at every meal of the day by the Egyptians—breakfast, lunch and supper. Bread was also an important part of the religious rituals of early Egypt. In fact, several of Egypt's Pharaohs were buried with loaves of bread in their tombs. In museums today, you can find 5,000-year-old loaves of bread preserved with the mummified bodies of Egyptian kings. The bread was placed as funerary offerings to nourish the kings on their journey to the afterlife (talk about stale!).

You can see how fundamentally important a baker's role was to Egyptian cuisine and religion. Archeological studies and research have shown that bakers in early Egypt made many types of bread. The Bible too tells us from the chief baker's dream that *"there were many kinds of bread in his basket"* (Genesis 40). Records show the bread produced had different shapes and sizes. Some bread was even shaped like animals in accordance with Egyptian deities. Research also shows that there were many different recipes for the bread with varying ingredients. They produced a wide range of bread products. The type of bread served to the king depended on the time of day, the occasion, and the climatic and religious seasons. So in essence, it was the baker's job to serve the king the right kind of bread in accordance with the season. With regard to kingdom building, a baker's role in a kingdom setting is to ensure that the king and the kingdom in general are doing the right thing in the right season.

We see the role of the baker being played out during the era of the Davidic kingdoms by the sons of Issachar who **"understood the times and seasons and what Israel ought to do"** (I Chronicles 12:32). The sons of Issachar advised the kingdom on what the season was and the appropriate mindset and action required for that season. We need men and women in our 21st century churches to advise the church on what it should be doing at a particular time. It is so easy to be doing the right thing at the wrong time. Many churches, businesses and families fall into this pitfall. For example, it is prudent and a wise thing for us to set aside money and save towards a goal. A saving habit is a good habit—it is the right thing to do. However, there are moments and seasons that call for sacrificial giving and supernatural seeding. If we remain in saving mode during such a season, we will miss an incredible opportunity to see a massive blessing in our lives.

Understanding times and seasons is a broad principle that covers all areas of kingdom building. There are seasons for churches to reach out, evangelize, and add new believers to the church. There are also seasons for the church to consolidate, disciple, and focus on equipping the saints. There are seasons for a business to expand and grow; but there are also seasons for a business to cut back and survive. King Solomon knew and understood this principle and tells us in Ecclesiastes, **"there is a time and season for everything under the sun"** (Ecclesiastes 3:1). The word *"season"* in this verse is derived from the Hebrew language, meaning **"an appointed time."** There are appointed times set by God for us, and it takes men of discernment (the bakers) to understand the times.

Even Satan knows about times and seasons

The Psalmist tells us, *"...like a tree planted by the*

*rivulets of water that **brings forth its fruit in its seasons...***" (Psalm 1:3). A tree does not bear fruit all year round but bears fruit at an appointed time. Imagine the frustration you would have if you thought that your mango tree bore fruit all year round. You would think you have a useless tree. Sometimes we are like that in our churches and businesses. Because we have no understanding of times and seasons, our expectations are not realistic; and this leaves us angry and bitter.

Even Satan knows about times and seasons—the Bible described, how after tempting Jesus, "*he waited for **an opportune time**" (Luke 4:13) to tempt him again. Satan knows that there are seasons where he is allowed to buffet us, tempt us, and sift us as wheat. During these times all we can do is stand and keep our faith. It is so sad to see Christians who do not understand times and seasons. They enter "sifting and wilderness seasons" and cast out and curse demons all day long in a desperate attempt to get out of their situations when what is really required is to stop "binding and loosing" and start standing strong to keep the faith. Do you see how much energy and resource can be lost when we do not understand times and seasons?

When you understand the season you are about to enter, you can prepare for it. Joseph told Pharaoh that there would be seven good years of rain followed by seven years of drought. Armed with this knowledge, Joseph and the Egyptians saved and stored food during the years of abundance, so that they would have enough food during the years of drought. You cannot adequately plan without understanding times and seasons. Walk into any business strategy meeting around the world, and the first thing people are trying to figure out is the condition and atmosphere of the upcoming seasons. They will then make their plans according to what they perceive the coming seasons will hold.

Kodak, one of the biggest companies in the world filed for bankruptcy in 2012, mainly because they failed to foresee the "season of the digital camera." Kodak needed a baker to advise them that the season of film technology was coming to an end and that the season of digital technology was upon them. The baker would have warned them, saying, "We need to cut spending on film and invest in digital."

The role of the baker is covered in Isaiah 50:4: *"The Lord GOD hath given me the tongue of the learned, **that I should know how to speak a word in season** to him that is weary..."* The baker knows the bread for the season. He knows what needs to be done—and when.

Chapter 6

Every Kingdom Needs a Butler

When the chief baker of Egypt was thrown in prison, he wasn't alone. The baker found himself in prison with the chief butler. Both had somehow managed to offend the king. Like the baker, the butler too had a dream that Joseph interpreted for him. Unlike the baker, though, the butler's dream had a happy ending which saw him reinstated to his position.

The butler had the important job of overseeing the king's palace. He was in charge of what the royal family ate and drank. He was in charge of what clothes they wore. He was in charge of the servants that served the king and queen. Because the butler was responsible for the king's food, he must have worked closely with the chief baker when deciding the king's menu. We do not know what they did to offend the king, but I can make a strong case that it had something to do with the food served to the king.

Now the butler was one of the few people who had inside access to the royal family. He interacted with them on a daily basis. He knew what they liked and disliked. He knew that the king liked his steak medium to well done, and that the queen preferred her eggs scrambled. He knew all the secrets of the royal family. He was the fly on the wall in the king's bedroom and the wall flower at the prince's parties. The butler was someone the royal family trusted with all their hearts. It is likely that members of the royal family confided in him and asked him advice on certain matters.

The butler was close to the king, and it is also likely that the king considered the butler more than a servant. The Bible alludes to this when we read about what happens when Pharaoh had his dreams.

> And it came to pass in the morning that his spirit was troubled; **and he sent and called for all the magicians of Egypt, and all the wise men thereof:** and Pharaoh told them his dream; but there was none that could interpret them unto Pharaoh. **Then spake the chief butler unto Pharaoh,** saying, I do remember my faults this day: Pharaoh was wroth with his servants, and put me in ward in the captain of the guard's house, both me and the chief baker: And we dreamed a dream in one night, I and he; we dreamed each man according to the interpretation of his dream. And there was there with us a young man, a Hebrew, servant to the captain of the guard; and we told him, and he interpreted to us our dreams; to each man according to his dream he did interpret.

And it came to pass, as he interpreted to us, so it was; me he restored unto mine office, and him he hanged. **Then Pharaoh sent and called Joseph, and they brought him hastily out of the dungeon...** (Genesis 41:8–14)

So we see that Pharaoh calls his inner circle to seek counsel on his dreams; he calls the wise men, the priests, the nobles, and princes of the land to a high-level confidential meeting. Three things stand out about this meeting that show the importance of the butler to the king:

1) Firstly, the butler is allowed into a highly classified meeting. I am sure the butler did not have the "security clearance" to be part of this meeting. Being part of this meeting shows the king trusted the butler with important matters.

2) Secondly, and more revealing, is the fact that the butler is allowed to speak at this meeting. This shows that the king held him in high regard.

3) The third point is most shocking of all—the king actually listens to him.

Butlers are kingdom influencers

We learn from this meeting that the butler influenced the outcome of the meeting. Butlers are kingdom influencers. Their closeness to the king allows them to earn the king's trust. They have the king's ear on all sorts of matters. I am sure that the more politically astute of Pharaoh's nobles and cabinet members probably used the butler to help push their agendas to the king. I too do this at times when I have an important meeting with other organizations; I try to identify the butler of the organization because I know that if we get the butler on our side he can influence the decision in our favor.

We can see this important role of the butler play out throughout the Scriptures. The first time we see this role is when Abraham learns that God intends to destroy the cities of Sodom and Gomorrah. This worries Abraham because his cousin Lot lives in this region. Abraham intercedes by going to God and asking Him if there is any way the destruction of the cities can be avoided. Ultimately, Abraham does not succeed in saving the two cities from destruction, but his influence is enough to provoke God to send a "rescue team" to bring out Lot and his family from the region before it was destroyed.

The role of the butler is even more evident in the dramatic life of King David. At one time, David was upset with his son Absalom. Absalom had murdered his half-brother Amnon, his father's eldest son—heir to the throne—for raping his sister.

We learn further that Absalom runs away from the kingdom to his grandfather, obviously fearing for his life. After three years, David finds it in his heart to finally forgive Absalom and *"his heart longs to see his son again"* (2 Samuel 13:39). At this point, Joab, the commander of David's army sees that David is longing for his son. Joab decides to help reconcile David to his son. But the thing I want to highlight is the manner in which Joab reconciles the two. Let us take up this family feud from 1 Samuel 14:1–3:

> *And Joab the son of Zeruiah saw that the king's heart was toward Absalom. And Joab sent to Tekoah* **and brought a wise woman** *from there. And he said to her, 'Please pretend yourself to be a mourner, and put on mourning clothes now, and do not anoint yourself with oil. But be like a woman who has mourned for the dead a long time.* **And come to the king, and speak in this way to him.' And Joab put the words in her mouth.**

We learn from reading further in this passage of Scripture that Joab succeeds in re-uniting David and Absalom. We know that Joab did not reconcile the two by directly getting involved, but we learn that he used the concept of the butler to influence the king's decision.

As we look at this Scripture closely, the first thing

we should ask ourselves is why Joab himself didn't go to the king. Joab was there with David from the beginning—in the cave at Adullam. They had fought many battles together. They had faced dangers and death together. They had eaten from the same table together many times for over thirty years. Joab was David's commander. Under Israeli law during the Davidic era, the commander of the army was the *de facto* second in rank to the king and would even rule provisionally when the king died until the eldest prince was installed as king by the priests. So Joab definitely had the rank and authority to speak to the king about almost anything. They had a long history together. So why didn't he go directly? Why send someone else? The answer lies in the fact that Joab knew that he did have a close (butler) relationship with David. They at one time had a good, healthy, professional relationship but because Joab in the past had directly disobeyed David's orders and gone against David's wishes on key matters, their relationship was fractious. Joab understood that the issue of David's son was "too sensitive" to bring up directly, so he indirectly created a "butler" moment using the woman from Tekoa.

We too must have similar discernment. We must understand when butler moments are needed. The twelve disciples also understood this; whenever, they wanted to bring up a sensitive issue to Jesus, they would ask it through Jesus' "butler"—*"the dis-*

ciple whom Jesus loved the most" (John 13:23).

Never overlook the role of the butler in a kingdom setting. His title and position may be insignificant in comparison to some of the more glorious titles and positions around, but his contribution is what sometimes makes the difference. Let me leave you with a recent example of how a "butler" saved the world:

In the 1960s, the world was on the brink of nuclear war. Russia and the USA were locked in a deadly game of "who blinks first." Historians and analysts have suggested that the world was "days and weeks" from full blown nuclear war. Those of us, who are old enough, remember the fear and uncertainty that gripped the world. Diplomacy had failed. Negotiations were on their last legs. There was tension, accusations and counter accusations. The only option left on the table for both countries seemed to be military confrontation. As a last ditch effort to avoid war, a close associate of the Russian president met in secret with a close associate of the American president. These men did not have official positions and titles in either government but were "mere" associates of their respective presidents. Their meeting formed the basis on which a deal was reached between both nations that saved the world from nuclear annihilation.

Isn't it paradoxical, that the butler of the US

President and the butler of the Russian President succeeded in saving the world, where the expert diplomats and government officials had failed? Similarly, Pharaoh's butler saved Egypt, when Pharaoh's experts had failed. The butler has an exceptional ability to open doors of opportunity where others cannot.

As butlers in the Kingdom of Heaven, we as Christians can influence the affairs of heavens. In John 15:14 Jesus tells His disciples, *"you are my friends."* There comes a time in our walk with Him, where He no longer considers us as servants but as friends. This happens to believers who spend consistent time in His presence, obey Him and please Him. Just like the butler spent twenty-four hours a day in Pharaoh's palace, pleased him and eventually won the king's confidence, we too, when we spend time with the King of kings, will be considered His friends. And as His friends, we can learn of the inner mysteries and secrets of His Kingdom. We are also in a privileged position to influence matters to work in our favor.

One of the most amazing aspects of being a friend of a king is that you do not have to go through all the layers of protocol and bureaucracy to speak to the king, but the king's door is always open to you. Isn't it amazing, that as friends of God, we have access to His throne when we desire? In the Old Testament, people had to sacrifice bulls and goats and go through the commanded laws to approach Him; but, today, as New Testament believers, we all have open access to His throne through the Lord Jesus Christ. It is such a privilege to be considered a friend of God—a privilege that all believers should desire.

Chapter Seven

Every Kingdom Needs a Cup-Bearer

Pharaoh's butler was a busy man. Besides performing the tasks of a butler, as we understand it in today's context, it seems that the butler was also the king's cup-bearer. When you read different versions of the Bible, the "butler" seemingly is given different titles. In most versions, he is referred to as the butler. In others he is referred to as the cup-bearer. In the ISV Bible, he is even referred to as the senior security officer. Talk about being multi-talented! Even though these are three different job descriptions, all of them had commonalities. Firstly, they required closeness to the king, and, secondly, they required a great amount of trust from the king. If the king did not trust you, you could not hold this post.

In Pharaoh's Egypt, a cup-bearer's duty was to serve drinks at the royal table. On account of constant fear of plots and conspiracies, the cup-bearer, as mentioned before had to be a trustworthy man. A cup-bearer's chief responsibility was to guard against poison in the king's cup, and sometimes he was required to swallow some of the wine in front of the king before serving it. As we said about the king-butler relationship, the confidential relationship between king and cup-bearer gave the cup-bearer a position of great influence.

The cup-bearer also had the responsibility to ensure that the wine served to the king was of the appropriate and desirable quality. The cup-bearer was the quality assuror. A cup-bearer is the one who is able to **determine the quality of a thing.** Every ministry, business, church, and country needs a cup-bearer that can say, "This is not a good wine; let's throw it out because if the kingdom drinks this, it will get drunk on cheap wine."

Every kingdom needs a system to monitor and evaluate the quality of *things* coming in and going out of the kingdom. A standard of excellence is essential in a kingdom setting because any *thing* that is of a high standard will transcend across generations. Quality control is a kingdom key and a significant part of why some products and companies have been in business for over a hundred years. They consistently strive to offer the best product and best company in the world.

Maintaining a standard of excellence requires effort, discipline and focus.

Maintaining a standard of excellence requires effort, discipline and focus. Ed Cole wrote, "It is easy to obtain, but it is harder to maintain." Many of us can start up churches and companies. But how many of us can maintain them and keep them running for hundreds of years so that our children's children inherit them? It is easy to get married, but it is much harder to stay married. It takes focused energy to maintain the quality of a *thing*.

Many Christians do not see the importance of maintaining quality in life and in living. Excellence is a spiritual principle. Many do not see excellence and a commitment to quality as being important to God. That is why when we visit the businesses and homes of some Christians, we are embarrassed to be associated with them because of the sloth and sub-standard lives they live. God cannot use many Christians today because many of us do not carry an excellent spirit.

When I read the Bible, I see that God considers excellence and quality very high on His priority list. When I read how He created man, I look at my body. My heart is beating; my ears, eyes, nose, and skin are all relaying messages to and from my brain. My red blood cells are carrying oxygen; my white blood cells are fighting infection. When God created me, He created an efficient high quality machine. When I look at creation—the earth and heavens—everything is perfect. God's work has a signature of excellence. God's work is so perfect that people often worship what He has created, instead of Him, the Creator. If God is meticulous in His work, we should arm ourselves with the same mindset.

The Bible instructs us in Romans 12:2 to, *"not be conformed to this world, but continually be transformed by the renewing of your minds so that we may determine what is the good, pleasing and* **perfect will of God.***"* God has a perfect will where He desires all of us to walk. Because the cup-bearer constantly tastes the wine—that is the spirit of a thing—he knows when we are not walking in the perfect will of God. Sometimes, believers will walk in the acceptable will of God but not His perfect will. Abraham did this when he had Ishmael. Ishmael was accepted before God, but he was not the perfect will.

When we walk in the perfect will of God, there is a blessing that is **commanded** over our calling. However, when we are walking in what is only acceptable, we will have to seek His blessing. Abraham sought a blessing from God for Ishmael, and God blessed him; but with Isaac—who was the perfect will—even though Abraham did seek a blessing, the child was blessed already. There was a commanded blessing spoken on Isaac before the earth was created. We see this pattern again years later when the children of Israel were wandering the desert for 40 years. It was not God's perfect will for them to wander in the desert, so Moses would have to constantly seek God's blessing over them; God did bless them with manna, water, meat, good health and clothes. But when the children of Israel eventually obeyed God and walked in His perfect will by crossing the Jordan into Canaan, they attracted the blessing onto themselves. The book of Joshua records how they conquered nation after nation that were far superior to themselves because they were living under the blessing.

It is so important to have cup-bearers in our lives because the cup-bearers will keep us in His perfect will and keep us in the commanded blessing. We must not be deceived and think that, just because God gives us "manna and meat," we are living in the commanded blessing. The commanded blessing belongs to those living in His perfect will. Sometimes, we get drunk on petty blessings and success. My wife is such an amazing cup-bearer to me—she keeps me in check. She challenges me and makes sure my motives for doing what I do are God-inspired. Anything less means I am stepping out from what is perfect, to what is only acceptable. This is why I believe that all Christians should have accountability partners that help them stay the course. The Apostle Paul was also a cup-bearer to his churches because he was always encouraging them to be **"sober-minded"** to **"check themselves to see if they are still in the faith,"** and not to **"dis-qualify"** themselves from the Kingdom of God (Titus 2:6).

The cup-bearer ensures we do not live below God's best. Sometimes in a kingdom setting, a cup-bearer is not a person or individual, but rather a system that helps maintain quality standards. For example, businesses that collect customer feedback about their products and services have a means to ascertain where they are. Also organizations that have a system of "checks and balances" can assess their progress. Organizations and individuals that do not have a cup-bearer in their make-up have predictable outcomes. They are inconsistent in their results; they do well for a season and then fade out. They will not last a long time. I said at the beginning of this chapter that cup-bearers help kingdoms to remain in place producing the same high quality results for generations. Inversely, the absence of cup-bearers ensures that the kingdom will eventually expire.

Finally, I believe that the ultimate cup-bearer is the Holy Spirit. The Bible shows us that He tells us when we are living below the required standard. Every believer should have Him close. Without the cup-bearer, every kingdom will flourish for a short while and then die. Every kingdom needs a cup-bearer to have the best that God has for it.

Chapter Eight

Every Kingdom Needs a Steward

When Joseph interpreted the king's dream and of-fered a solution to the conundrum in which the king found himself, the king decided there was none better than Joseph himself to oversee this whole operation. So Pharaoh appointed Joseph second in rank in the whole land. Problem solv-ers always get the best jobs. In a couple of hours, Joseph was promoted from prison to the second highest office in the land. Many people see this re-markable promotion in Joseph and pray that God will take them from zero to hero "just like that." People who have this prayer of accelerated promo-tion in their lives are in danger of being called "wishful dreamers."

It is important to note that Joseph was not pro-moted "just like that." If you look carefully at his life, you will see he was a faithful steward from when he was a young boy. There was a consistency in Joseph's life. As a boy, he was faithful in his re-sponsibilities over his father's affairs. As a slave in Egypt, he was faithful in his responsibilities over Potiphar's household. As a prisoner, he was faith-ful in his responsibilities over the prison warden's jail. Because Joseph was faithful with the few given to him, he could be trusted with plenty.

Stewards are managers and their role is administrative.

In our church you will not get promoted "just like that." All our leaders have a track record of serving and faithfulness. We value stewardship in our church. The Bible says this about stewardship, *"For though I preach the gospel, no glory is to me. For necessity is laid on me; yea, woe is to me if I do not preach the gospel! For if I do this willingly, I have a reward; but if against my will, I have been entrusted with a stewardship"* (I Corinthians 9:17, NKJV). The King James Version says it in this manner, *"For if I do this thing willingly, I have a reward: but if against my will,* a **dispensation** *of the gospel* **is committed unto me.**" The word 'dispensation' in the Greek language is the word *oikonomia*, meaning administration (of a household or estate). The word *oikonomia* is derived from the word *oikonomo* meaning a manager or overseer. Stewardship means being a manager or overseer of a domain given to you even if you are not naturally inclined and willing to accept it. Joseph did not want to be in Potiphar's house; he did not want to be in prison; but while he was there, he executed the responsibilities given to him with care and diligence. A steward manages the affairs of another. He is responsible for the day-to-day running of an organization.

We know that Potiphar "did not concern himself with anything to do with his household" because he knew that it was taken care of by Joseph, his steward (Genesis 39:6). Potiphar was able to focus wholly on what he needed to do without the "distraction" of running a household. Sometimes, as kings and leaders in our organizations, we get so embroiled in the everyday details of running an organization that we no longer focus on **leading** the organization—instead we become **managers**. Kings are the vision carriers of a kingdom—their role is apostolic and strategic. Stewards are managers and their role is administrative. Stewards give kings the freedom to lead effectively.

I know many church pastors who are stuck in the leadership versus management conundrum. Because they get involved in the day-to-day running of the church, the message they preach on a Sunday is not as effective as it once was. The daily hassles of running the church keep them from attending to the ministry of the word. A man of God should stick to his calling—he should be the pastor, teacher, or apostle and leave the administrative duties to others.

Moses set a great example for us by delegating responsibilities to those who were faithful and loyal around him. If as a king, you are still involved in the day-to-day details of your kingdom, you will burn out—that is inevitable. A burned out king is a king who is vulnerable to attacks from the enemy. When a man of God falls from grace, look at the pattern of his life in the months preceding his fall. One of the things you will find is that he was tired and burned out from carrying too big a load. This is why Moses' father-in-law warned him saying, *"The thing you are doing is not good... you will soon wear yourself out... delegate some of your load to faithful men..."* (Exodus 18:17–18).

Without stewards, a kingdom will soon find itself in debt. Stewards are good treasurers—they keep excellent financial records. The Proverbs say, *"Be thou diligent to know the state of thy flocks, and look well to thy herds."* (Proverbs 27:23). A steward will know the financial state of the kingdom at all times. Without stewards, skilled labor and personnel would soon leave the kingdom. Stewards are excellent man-managers. Luke 16 tells us of the unjust steward. Even though he was dishonest, he was still a good man-manager because he used his good relationships with people to get out of trouble.

Without stewards, kingdoms would not have accurate knowledge of significant events; history would be lost. Stewards keep timely and detailed records of events. In the Old Testament, scribes were high ranking officials in the king's inner circle. Their job was to journal important events happening in the kingdom. It would be imprudent to run a kingdom without a steward.

We are stewards of God's gospel. God has given us that responsibility. We are responsible for the day-to-day administration of His gospel here on earth. This is an important mindset to have. When Moses was with the children of Israel in the wilderness, the people began to complain to Moses because of the hardships they were enduring. The people even discussed killing Moses and returning to Egypt. When Moses heard the rumors, he cried to God, reminding Him, "God, **these are your people, not mine. You called me to lead them, I did not ask for this.** *If you are going to treat me like this, remove me as leader of Israel...*" (Numbers 11:15). Moses knew he was a steward of God's people. They were not his people, but God's. Moses knew that the ultimate responsibility to lead the people out of trouble lay with God—not him. He reminded God that the power belonged to Him and that if He didn't intervene, Israel would be destroyed in the wilderness, and the Lord's name would be dishonored. Moses knew God would never let that happen.

When we come before God in a similar disposition, we can seek His help reminding Him saying, "God this is not my church—it is Your church!" "God, this is not my business, it is Your business."

God cannot allow what is His to fail. But because of greed, many believers have taken what they have been given stewardship over as their own possession. This is a dangerous place to be because Christ warns us, saying, *"A man with great possessions will struggle to enter the Kingdom of God"* (Matthew 19:24). I always tell my church that, if God blesses you with great wealth, you are a steward of that wealth; be a good steward of that wealth; grow it; create even more wealth, but remember you are a steward over those resources. As a steward, if God asks you to give away those resources, you will, because you know it doesn't belong to you, but God. However, if you see yourself as the possessor of those resources, you will struggle to obey Him when He asks you to be liberal.

In the Holy Trinity, The Holy Spirit is identified as the Chief Administrator. When Jesus Christ was lifted up to the Heavens to sit at the right hand of the Father, He promised that the Holy Spirit would be left here with us to be with us on a daily basis as our Comforter, Helper, Counselor, Friend, Encourager, Intercessor. The Holy Spirit is Heaven's steward. If the Kingdom of Heaven sees fit to have a steward on its team, it is also important to have a steward on our teams.

Chapter Nine

Every Kingdom Needs Laborers

Every kingdom needs people who can roll up their sleeves, work up a sweat and not be afraid to get their hands dirty. Laborers are the builders of the kingdom. The Bible shows that God is a worker. He worked when He created the Heavens and Earth and *"rested on the seventh day from **His work"*** (Genesis 2:2). Jesus says in John, ***"the work** I see My Father doing, I do likewise"* (John 5:19). The Father and Son are working right now. Work is a spiritual principle, and, without it, nothing would be accomplished in life. The Bible tells us *"we are **co-workers** with Him"* (2 Corinthians 6:1). Again it says *"we are **fellow workers** for the Kingdom of God"* (I Corinthians 3:9). God expects us to work. He wants us to work with Him in building His Kingdom. The Psalmist says, *"Unless the Lord builds the house, the builders build in vain"* (Psalm 127:1). Laborers build under the direction of the king. Jesus did work only **after** seeing what the Father was working on.

Laborers turn the king's vision into reality. Laborers might not see and understand the full vision, but each individual laborer has a part to play to complete the picture. We see this in the book of

Nehemiah, where different families were asked to repair different sections of the wall. Each family worked on a section allocated to them, but as each one finished their part, the whole wall started to become complete. Laborers are important to a kingdom because they bring completion. This is why the enemy will consistently attack your workers. The enemy understands that, without workers, the work cannot be complete. This is what the enemy tried to do with Nehemiah's workers. He would attack them to slow down their work. Workers cannot protect themselves because they do not carry weapons of war but rather tools of the trade. Workers need the king's protection and cover. Kings need to protect their workers. Without this protection, the workers would be constantly harassed by the enemy.

Workers need the king's protection and cover.

During the Second World War, one of the high priority targets for both sides was to destroy factories and transportation systems in various cities to incapacitate the workforce of the enemy. Without a workforce, the enemy's capability to reproduce bombs and machinery is limited. Today, one of the key indicators of the health of a country's economy is its unemployment rate. If a country has high unemployment, it means a significant percentage of people are unproductive. An unproductive kingdom is a dying kingdom. Jesus requires us as Christians to be productive. God will *dig out and cut off trees* that are not productive. I know you have probably heard this statement from many a politician: the workforce is the backbone of the nation. Though abused by politicians, this statement is true. Jesus knew this and said, *"Pray for laborers"* (Matthew 9:38). Laborers are the backbone of the Kingdom of God. Laborers are the ones who will go in the field and harvest the wheat. Laborers sow the seed. When Jesus walked on earth in the flesh, He Himself did not go to the four corners of the world to preach and disciple the nations. He left the mandate to me and you—the laborers.

The word "work" is not preached as much as it should be in the 21st century church. Young people do not value work as much as the "old timers" did. There are now methods and means that have been invented to avoid work. Think about it—the microwave, remote controls, audio books, ten steps to prosperity conferences—all these were invented to reduce the amount of work a human being has to do. Yes, of course, some of it is invented in the name of efficiency and effectiveness, but I think I can say our generation is the laziest generation ever. We make more money on less work. We are building skyscrapers on a shaky foundation. No wonder the world's financial system is in turmoil. A lot of money was made with very little work involved. We must encourage our young people to value work. They must know that hard work is their ticket.

We must not be ashamed to be seen as laborers. God Himself is a worker. We are not higher than God, and we should not see laboring as an unimportant task for inferior people. Work is a privilege and an honor. King Solomon in his old age reflected the most important things in life. As a king who was the richest man in the world and had the most beautiful wives and lived the most glamorous life, his conclusion to what is important in life is a humbling one and is captured in this Scripture, *"Therefore I have seen **that there is nothing better than that a man should rejoice in his own works for that is his portion;** for who can bring him to see what shall be after him?"* (Ecclesiastes 3:22). Work given to us by God is our portion. We should rejoice in it. If a king gives you work, this is your inheritance, so work.

The Apostle Paul knew all about laboring. He stated, *"**we work day and night** so that I will not be a burden to any"* (I Thessalonians 2:9, ISV). Paul did spiritual work during the day—preaching and ministering the gospel, but he also did physical labor during the night too—building tents to support his livelihood. The Bible records Paul having a handkerchief that healed the sick when they were in contact with it. This hankie had his sweat from his work. His sweat brought healing to a city. Our labor brings healing to a kingdom. Paul also instructed the church saying, *"Work with your hands so that you may eat"* (2 Thessalonians 3:10). Labor feeds a kingdom. Margaret Thatcher, Prime Minister of Great Britain for ten years in the eighties, actually formed an economic policy based on this passage of Scripture. Her thinking was simplistic; but it worked because in the mid-eighties, Great Britain went through an economic boom that had not been seen for some time. Her policy was to create jobs for all Britons; more jobs equals higher productivity; higher productivity equals higher GDP. Labor brings prosperity to a kingdom.

Let me close this chapter with a graphic illustration of the power of work. Jesus went to the Mount of Olives to pray. He knew His time was upon Him. Luke 22:44 describes this time of prayer saying, *"And being in an agony He prayed more earnestly. And His sweat was as it were great drops of blood falling down to the ground."* Sweat is a result of work. Jesus worked His way to the Cross. The Bible tells us that *"ALL labor leads to a reward"* (Proverbs 14:23). The reward of Jesus' work was salvation to all mankind. A kingdom that has laborers is a kingdom that is rewarded.

Chapter Ten

Every Kingdom Needs a Prison Warden

Prison is a terrible place to be. If you have ever been incarcerated, you know what I am talking about. You could share your prison cell with murderers and rapists—sadistic men who give no thought to the value of life. Prison can be a lawless place because it is filled with lawless men. There must be prison wardens to enforce order and discipline. A warden's job is an unpredictable one—today is ordinary, tomorrow a riot breaks out. A warden must be prepared all the time.

The Bible tells us that in any setting, *"there are vessels of honor and vessels of dishonor"* (2 Timothy 2:20). In your kingdom there are good people who contribute to the advancement of the kingdom; there are also evil and bad people who *"will not sleep until they have done evil"* (Proverbs 4:16). It is the job of the warden to ensure that there is order in the kingdom. The warden is the enforcer. Anything that is out of alignment, the warden needs to bring back into alignment. God is a God of order. He does not operate in chaos. I have been to companies and organizations where chaos is the order of the day. The head does not know what the toe is doing. Chaos and disorder are kingdom killers. When God wanted to destroy the Tower of Babel, He brought chaos and confusion to the people, and soon the work stopped.

Division is the number one killer of kingdoms.

Chaos, disorder, and confusion are also weapons used by our enemies to bring down our kingdoms. Christ taught that a house that is divided cannot stand. Division is the number one *killer* of kingdoms. Many churches, businesses, and organizations have fallen because of divided opinions. Paul warns clearly in the Bible, *"saying dogs and wolves will come amongst you"* (Acts 20:29). He warns us several times telling us that false brethren and prophets will come. He warns us of divisive people who will come into our kingdoms. Their main objective is to break our kingdoms apart. I want to give you a guarantee—these people are in your organization. They are in your church right now. They are in your business right now. For some, they could be in your family. I say these things because the Word of God tells me. When you look at your church congregants in your next meeting, know that you have a few bad wolves in sheep's clothing. Paul warns us that they will come in secretly. They will use deceit and cunning to split your kingdom apart. Do not be naïve and ignorant of the enemy's tactics. The warden is key to keeping your kingdom together.

Let's look at the Scriptures. Every time the Pharisees and Sadducees tried to use deceit and cunning as a means to trap Jesus, He would "perceive in His spirit" that their motivation was to harm Him (Mark 2:8). I said before that wardens must be prepared all the time; they must be able to discern and identify the hidden motives of the unworthy vessels in your kingdom. When he identifies them, the warden must expose them. Secret enemies hate being discovered. They hate the light. The warden brings light in dark areas. Transparency is an important part of the kingdom. Look at your kingdom closely. If there is any area that is not clear, any area that is grey or cloudy, shine your light in this area; you will be surprised at the hidden motives and agendas you find.

In Africa, there are many business deals done over coffee and in take-away places. These deals are not protected by written and signed agreements. If you are in such an agreement, you are not protected; the warden cannot help you. There is a saying: **what is not written does not exist!** Jesus is real because He is the Word, and the Word is written. Many conflicts have arisen because of unwritten agreements. People disagree, and there is no document to reference in order to enforce and bring into alignment the agreement and hold the party that broke the terms accountable. Having a warden mentality ensures that your kingdom is protected against threats that can destroy it. Sometimes we give our enemies too much opportunity to destroy us. Let us have wardens in our kingdoms to keep honest people honest. Loopholes and grey areas tempt even the most honest person to be dishonest because he knows he is covered by the darkness.

We know and have read stories of how millions of dollars have *"disappeared"* from bank accounts. How does a million dollars disappear? The answer is that it is easy for it to disappear when the warden is not part of a kingdom. The warden promotes transparency and accountability. He always promotes law and order in a kingdom. The Bible records a time when there was no warden in the kingdom of Israel. It was the time when the generation of Joshua had passed on, and the children of Israel did not know nor follow the Lord. The Bible states that the people of Israel ***"did what was right in their own eyes"*** (Judges 17:6, NKJV). There was no rule of law, and there was no-one to enforce the law. It was during this time that we learn that men blatantly disregarded each other and treated each other with such malevolent acts that people who heard of these acts were outraged. Two incidents stand out during this lawless era.

    1.) The first one is from Judges 17, with a man called Micah from Mount Ephraim. This man had stolen money from his mother and lived a cursed life because his mother had cursed "whoever" had stolen the money. The man would repent later but would then "hire" a Levite to be his "personal" priest in his own home. Can you see the level of chaos and disorder in this story? Levites were meant to serve the whole nation in the tent of meeting, but this particular Levite had left his post and allowed himself to be hired as a priest and build his owner "another" place of worship. Also Levities were not ordained to be priests but to serve the priests in the Sanctuary. Such things were unheard of in Israel. We then learn that a small band of men from the tribe of Dan would pass through Micah's house and steal the priest for themselves.

2.) The second incident is from Judges 19, where a Levite from Mount Ephraim marries a concubine. Again this is a picture of disorder. Levites were instructed to marry virgins according to the Law. This concubine then has an extra-marital affair—another picture of disorder. The Levite would then find out and send his concubine away. This is another disregard for God's Law because the Law instructed that those who committed adultery were to be stoned. Eventually, the Levite forgives his concubine and goes to her father's house to bring her back to his house. On the way back she is raped by a group of lawless men. This incident sparks a national outrage that leads to civil war between the tribes of Israel. The war claimed close to a 100,000 lives. Can you see the level of lawlessness and disorder?

Can you see what happens when there is no warden in the kingdom? Everyone does what they want without fear of prosecution. The law is disregarded, and everyone takes the law into their own hands. Chaos is the order of the day. Samuel the judge would then come along years later and eventually bring order, but so much had been lost by Israel. The Ark was lost. Israel lived in bondage from its enemies. Their tribes were divided. There are so many nations, churches, businesses, and even families that have similar chaotic situations to the stories in Judges 17 and 19.

God does not want chaos for us. He does not want our kingdoms to be in disorder. We must allow the warden to do his job in the kingdom. *"When the righteous rule in a nation, the people rejoice. But when the wicked rule, the people live in bondage"* (Proverbs 29:2).

Chapter Eleven

Every Kingdom Needs Advisers

Before Israel crossed the Jordan River into Canaan, the nation was nomadic in nature. They moved from place to place without ever staying in one place for very long. This was true from the time of Abraham to the days of Moses. Israel was structured according to tribal lines with the each tribe appointing a head and elders to govern it. The elders of each tribe were responsible for the day to day details of their respective tribe. Each tribe had complete autonomy in specific areas like military organization, job professions, and affairs related to the basic welfare of tribe members. The Bible shows us the distinct differences between the tribes in several places. It describes the tribe of *"Benjamin as being skilled with the bow and sling, and could shoot using their left and right hands"* (I Chronicles 12:2). The tribe of Gad were *"specialists in using the shield and buckler"* (I Chronicles 12:8). The sons of Issachar were skilled in understanding the times. The sons of Zebulun were skilled military strategists, and the sons of Naphtali were skilled in using the spear. The twelve tribes were always geographically in the same place, dwelling in tents, so in times of war it was easier for them to combine their skills and fight which made them a strong unit. Food and water were almost always supernaturally provided by the Lord. They didn't farm or hunt or work to produce a food supply.

All of this changed when they began to possess the "promised land." They began to live in cities and towns. The tribes now lived in different geographical locations. Bringing the nation together for war or for the commanded gatherings were now logistically more challenging. They also had to farm and grow their own crops and fruits. The towns and cities needed water supplies. For the first time, Israel had a border, and this border needed to be defended. Governing Israel after the Jordan River crossing was much more complicated and complex than before. There were a plethora of issues and situations that needed to be governed and managed effectively. The style of government changed to a more centralized form of government. The tribes had less autonomy, and more powers were given to the leader of Israel. The leader of Israel needed more help in running the country. It was at this time that the leaders and kings of Israel began to create official positions for senior advisors in the government.

Advisors to the king were men and women who had deep understanding and knowledge about a topic or matter. The king would draw from this well of knowledge when he needed to make important decisions. The advisor's role was to provide the king with information and facts that would be relevant in helping the king make a decision. As a king, it is impossible for you to know everything there is to know about building a kingdom. You will need people around you who are experts in their respective fields. In fact, the Bible shows us that *"those who think they are wise and know everything are actually fools"* (Proverbs 26:12). God shows us that *"in the abundance of counsel, there is victory"* (Proverbs 11:14). A king who has many advisors in his government or leadership structure will succeed. A king who feels he is the wisest and most knowledgeable in the kingdom will eventually experience failure. His weaknesses will be perpetuated throughout the kingdom. Advisors in the kingdom cover up a king's weakness. In areas where the king is weak, advisors who are experts in that field will cover the gaps. A humble king will always listen to their counsel. A proud king will ignore sensible counsel to his ruin. Though a simple principle, many have ignored it, leading them to ruin their families, businesses, and churches. Think about it. Husbands, how many times have you found yourself in a difficult place after ignoring your wife's concerns about a business deal? Or as CEO, you find your company in trouble after ignoring your accountant's advice. Every time you are defeated, look back and analyze the counsel you received. Almost ten times out of ten, you will find you ignored or disregarded the advice of others.

Kingdoms that create forums for debate will always be a step ahead of those that have closed channels of communication.

Kings should be prepared to sometimes hear very difficult counsel from their advisors. It is very healthy for advisors to sometimes disagree with their kings. As long as the advisors are fully convinced and can build a case for their argument, disagreements and differences in opinion will lead to open debate that will form the basis of lasting solutions on the debated topic. Kingdoms that create forums for debate will always be a step ahead of those that have closed channels of communication. A king who closes himself from hearing criticism or a king that does not handle criticism well will surround himself with "yes" men. These are men who will agree with the king over everything and anything, even if they know it is wrong. "Yes" men will destroy a kingdom. "Yes" men will allow a country to go war, when they know that there are avenues of peace still available. "Yes" men will allow their pastor to make erroneous decisions, knowing too well the disastrous outcome to follow.

King Ahab was one such king who surrounded himself with "yes" men. He wanted God's prophets to only declare the things that made him feel good. Any prophet who declared otherwise was arrested or executed by the king. King Ahab's refusal to listen to Godly counsel expressed in the Bible in 1 Kings 22 eventually led him to his death. The Apostle Paul warns us that there will come a time *"when people only want to hear things that make them feel nice and tickles their ears"* (2 Timothy 4:3). Scripture also warns us stating, *"Be careful when all men speak well of you"* (Luke 6:26). If you are a leader and people around you ALWAYS speak well of you, then there are two possible reasons why. First reason is that you are Superman. The second reason is that you are surrounded by "yes" men. Since we know Superman is confined to the pages of comic books, the second reason, almost always holds true to most situations. Harry Truman, a former U.S. president, once said, "The President is always abused. If he isn't, he isn't doing anything." I have learned to embrace constructive criticism and to receive counsel that is not easy to receive. This has developed me as a person and has developed our church. The Bible has a name for people who cannot receive counsel. It calls them "stiff-necked." Stiff-necked people are not teachable. An unteachable person cannot develop and progress because he has reached the end of learning.

From studying the Scriptures, it has been revealed to us that our Lord is also Counselor to us. Isaiah 9:6 says, *"For to us a Child is born, to us a Son is given; and the government shall be on His shoulder; and His name shall be called Wonderful,* **Counselor**, *The mighty*

God, *The everlasting Father, The Prince of Peace.*" It says again in Psalm 106:13, "*They hurried and forgot His works; they did not wait for His* **counsel**."

> *I counsel you to buy from Me gold purified by fire, so that you may be rich; and white clothing, so that you may be clothed, and so that the shame of your nakedness does not appear. And anoint your eyes with eye salve, so that you may see* (Revelation 3:18).

The word "counsel" in Hebrew is the word "ay-tsaw'" meaning "to plan or to be prudent or to purpose." When we follow His Counsel, we are following His perfect plan and purpose in any situation. This is the highest level that any believer can live at. All of God's Commandments and Laws are written plainly in black and white in the Bible. However, His Counsel is revealed to us by spending time with Him through Christ and being filled by the Holy Spirit. Paul and the early church were eager to lay their hands on and have all Christians filled with the Holy Spirit because this gave Christians access to His Counsel and allowed them to live at a higher dimension.

Remember the incident Jesus had with the rich young ruler. This young ruler felt a hole in his life, so he went and asked the Lord, "*Good Teacher, what shall I do to inherit eternal life?*" Jesus answered Him saying:

You know the commandments: *Do not commit adultery, do not kill, do not steal, do not bear false witness, honor your father and your mother." The ruler answered Jesus back saying, "I have* **kept** *all these from my youth up." Then Jesus* **counseled** *the ruler saying, "Yet you lack one thing. Sell all that you have and distribute to the poor, and you shall have treasure in Heaven. And come, follow Me"* (Luke 18:22).

We can see that the ruler had kept and lived according to the Law from his childhood. Despite keeping the Law "religiously," this ruler knew in his heart that he was living below his fullest potential. Jesus saw this and hence invited him to move from the realm of the Law into the realm of His counsel. If this ruler had accepted and received the counsel of the Lord, he would have lived a fulfilled life. We as believers must strive to live in His counsel.

If God sees fit to Counsel His Kingdom subjects, we too must consider it important to have advisors in our governmental structures. In the abundance of counsel, we can wage war and have victory. In my family and church, I desire to have wise advisors around me because I know that I will rack up more points in the victories column and the defeat column will decrease.

Chapter Twelve

Every Kingdom Needs Garment Makers

Peter and the other disciples sat around the fire with the Lord Jesus Christ. They had just eaten a wonderful breakfast of "barbecued" fish. Peter and the disciples were still a little bit shocked. Just a few weeks ago, they had seen Jesus beaten, flogged, and crucified on the cross. They had seen Him breathe His last breath and die. They had seen Him buried and had seen the Roman soldiers roll the big stone to seal the tomb. But here He was, sitting with them and eating fish. It seemed so surreal to the disciples. The Scriptures show us that the disciples were even afraid to say anything to him. However, Jesus spoke first by instructing Peter "to feed His sheep." Jesus then said this to Peter, *"Truly, truly, I say to you, When you were young, you **girded yourself and walked where you wished**. But when you grow old, you shall stretch forth your hands and another **shall gird you and carry you where** you **do not wish**"* (John 21:18).

This statement from Jesus was not just prophetic in its nature but it was also analogous. Jesus was describing the nature of Peter's calling and task in His Kingdom using an illustration that insinuated Peter's task and purpose in the Kingdom would be determined by the type of garments given to him to wear. Jesus understood that a man's job or task in a kingdom could be identified by the garments he wore. Soldiers, tax collectors, blacksmiths, priests, and various other professionals could be identified by the garments they wore. What Jesus was saying to Peter, was that, if my "garment makers" dress you in a "physician's attire," your purpose in this season is to heal. If my "garment makers" dress you in a "soldier's attire," your purpose in the season is to fight. Jesus was saying, **"You will know your purpose and task for the season by the garments given to you."** I said in the beginning of this book that every subject in a kingdom has a task and role to fulfill. Garment makers in a kingdom make garments or mantles that subjects can wear that help subjects in that kingdom to understand their role. Understanding your calling or role in life can be a challenging and complex affair; but if "another" dresses you, you will be able to determine, by the nature of the dress, your area of responsibility.

A good example of a "garment maker" who I feel brings out the role of a garment maker in the 21st century setting is the man Barnabas. Barnabas saw the gift on Saul's life and, not only encouraged Saul, but also helped "pave" the way for him to operate in his calling. Saul had just been born again after the encounter with the Lord on the road to Damascus. After the encounter, Saul could sense the "call of God" on his life. He knew God had called him to something big, but he didn't what, where, and, most importantly, how he would fulfill this call. As followers of Christ, many of us have experienced what Saul was experiencing— that we are called to something significant but have little insight and understanding to the thing we are called. Barnabas helped Saul by identifying his gifting and calling. Remember, one of the key characteristics of garment makers is that they give identity to kingdom subjects. Because of Barnabas, most of the other disciples who had been suspicious of Saul began to recognize and see the call of God on Saul's life. I don't know if you have ever met a person like Barnabas—a person who can see things in you, which you yourself cannot see; a person who is able to draw the gifting and anointing out of you; a person who makes it easier for you to walk in your calling.

As a pastor of a large church, one of the hardest tasks to accomplish is organizing and coordinating the gifts and talents available to the church. There are so many people in our church who are super-gifted and super-talented; and, sometimes, it is not easy to know what to do with these gifts. This is why we need garment makers in the church. They help bring order because everyone will have their roles and responsibilities identified by the garment maker. With garment makers available to us, the church can work together as a coordinated unit.

A biblical pattern for building church structures is given to us in Ephesians 4:13–16, with God instructing us that the church should be structured according to the gifts available to the body:

> *And truly He gave some to be apostles, and some to be prophets, and some to be evangelists, and some to be pastors and teachers,* **for the perfecting of the saints, for the work of the ministry, for the edifying of the body of Christ. And this until we all come into the unity of the faith and of the knowledge of the Son of God, to a full-grown man, to the measure of the stature of the fullness of Christ;** *so that we no longer may be infants, tossed to and fro and carried about by every wind of doctrine, in the dishonesty of men, in cunning craftiness, to the wiles of deceit. But that you, speaking the truth in love, may in all things grow up to Him who is the Head, even Christ;* **from whom the whole body, fitted together and compacted by that which every joint supplies, according to the effectual working in the measure of each part, producing the growth of the body to the edifying of itself in love.**

When all the gifts available to the body of Christ are coordinated effectively, it edifies the church; and the church becomes an effective fruitful unit. You can see that, without garment makers, it would be difficult to effectively coordinate all the gifts together. This is also true for any organization or business. In the business world, garment makers can be known as talent scouts or head-hunters.

A man must be worthy of the garments he wears.

When we do not wear the correct garments for our calling, it brings confusion to the body. God is greatly displeased when we wear garments of our own choosing and ignore the garments especially made for us. A person who does this is a deceitful person. His outward appearance is counterfeit. Have you ever appointed someone to a position in your organization only to discover that person was the wrong person for the job? If you have, you were probably deceived by their outward appearance. A man must be worthy of the garments he wears. Military people worldwide are taught to wear their uniform with pride. God also expects us to be worthy of the garments He gives us to wear. He illustrates this in the parable of the king who held a wedding banquet for his son:

> And the king coming in to look over the guests, **he saw a man there who did not have on a wedding garment.** And he said to him, 'Friend, how did you come in here without having a wedding garment?' And he was speechless. Then the

king said to the servants, 'Bind him hand and foot and take him away, and cast him into outer darkness. There shall be weeping and gnashing of teeth.' For many are called, but few chosen (Matthew 22:13, 14).

God wants us to be dressed appropriately for our calling. He calls us, but we determine whether we are chosen by accepting the garments given to us.

When Joseph was in his father's house, he was given a coat of many colors. When he was in Potiphar's house, he was given the garment of slaves. When he was in prison, he had prison clothes, and, finally, when he was Vizier of Egypt, he wore the garments of kings. God also gave specific instruction on the design of Aaron's garments for entering into the Holy of Holies. Aaron could not enter into His Presence dressed as he pleased. He had to be dressed in the garments given to him by the Garment Maker. In conclusion, the Bible encourages us to *"put on Christ"* (Galatians 3:27). When we put on Christ, we are presentable to stand before God, in His very Presence. Like Aaron, if we haven't put on the "garment of Christ", our enemies have a legitimate right to oppose us. Satan and his demons can see the dress we put on. If we are not dressed appropriately, he will stand accusing us. Look at Zechariah 3:1–5:

Then I saw Joshua the High Priest standing in

*the presence of the angel of the LORD, **with Satan standing at his right to oppose him.** The LORD told Satan, "The LORD rebuke you, Satan—in fact, may the LORD who has chosen Jerusalem rebuke you! This man is a burning brand plucked from the fire, is he not? Now Joshua **was wearing filthy clothes** as he stood in the presence of the angel. So the angel continued to tell those who were standing in his presence, **"Remove his filthy clothes."** And he told Joshua, **"Look how I've removed your iniquity. Now I'm clothing you with fine garments."** Then I said, **"Let them place a pure diadem on his head." So they placed the pure diadem on his head and clothed him with fine garments** while the angel of the LORD was standing beside them.*

Isn't it wonderful that our God removes the filthy garments we have and replaces them with royal clothing? I love to believe that when we have put on Christ, Satan and his demons no longer see us. We become identified with Christ and are hidden in Him. So when Satan sees us, he sees Christ. And when he sees Christ, he trembles.

Chapter Thirteen

Every Kingdom Needs Protectors

Israel was at war—again. It was the old enemy Philistine. King David for the umpteenth time led his army out to battle. David was not a young man any more. He had been king for many years now and had many glorious victories under his belt. But now, his aging muscles were not as quick and nimble as before. In his youth, he was the greatest warrior alive; but now, most of his army was equally as good as him—if not better. 2 Samuel 21:15–17 depicts this particular battle:

> *And again the Philistines warred with Israel. And David went down, and his servants with him, and fought against the Philistines. **And David became faint.** And Ishbi-benob, who was of the sons of the giant, the weight of whose spear was three hundred shekels of bronze in weight, he being girded with a new sword, **thought to kill David.** But Abishai the son of Zeruiah **came to his aid,** and struck the Philistine, and killed him. Then the men of David swore to him, saying, **You shall not go out to battle with us any more, so that you do not put out the light of Israel.***

We can see that David would have probably been

killed if Abishai had not come to the rescue. Abishai protected the king from harm. Abishai, not only saved the king's life, but by saving the king, he also saved the nation. To some, this might seem like an over-exaggeration; but the fact is that David was the vision carrier of the nation. Without him, there would be no vision. As previously stated–where there is no vision, the people perish. This is why we need protectors—they protect the vision carriers in a kingdom.

The enemy will always attempt to eliminate the kings and vision carriers in the kingdom. During His time on earth, Jesus had several attempts on His life. His disciples, too, suffered greatly with imprisonments and beatings and survived several murderous plots. If you are a king or vision carrier, you are probably high on Satan's hit-list. The threat to the king is real; he needs to be protected. The king's family should also be included in the ring of protection. Today, countries around the world spend millions of dollars protecting their Presidents because they understand that once the head is cut off, the whole nation is vulnerable. King David knew this, too, and he included a "Secret Service" type protective team in his military to protect himself and the royal family. The two teams responsible for the security of the family were the Cherethites and Pelethites. The Cherethites were highly skilled assassins that were the security detail of the royal family. The word "Cherethite" means "life guardsman" in its original Hebrew language. The Cherethites protected the king with their lives. They would rather die than see harm come to the king. The Cherethites were not only there for the king's protection, but they were his "hit squad" that reported directly to the king. The Pelethites were not as militant as the Cherethites but their role was just as important. They were more of couriers and messengers and ensured that the "trustworthy" information flowed to and from the king. Benaiah, the son of Johoiada, a fierce and valiant warrior was the commander of the Cherethites and Pelethites. Assassinating the king during David's and Solomon's reign was not an easy task. Surprisingly, the Cherethites and Pelethtites are not mentioned again in the Bible after the death of Solomon. It seems that succeeding kings in Israel did not value "protecting the vision" as much as David did. Subsequently, because of this attitude, we learn from the Bible that at least four kings of Israel were assassinated in attempted *coups d'états.*

David saw the need to form this protective ring around him during his days on the run from King Saul. Since there was a bounty on his head and every soldier under King Saul's command wanted the honor of killing him, there was a need for David to be protected. He was the future and light of Israel. David also probably had heard of what had happened to Mephibosheth, the son of Jonathan, David's friend. *"Meanwhile, Saul's son Jonathan had a son whose feet were crippled. When he was five years old, news had arrived about Saul and Jonathan from Jezreel,* **and his nurse picked him up to flee,** *but in her hurry to leave, he happened to fall and became lame. His name was Mephibosheth"* (2 Samuel 4:4). What was a prince of Israel doing only in the presence of a nurse? Shouldn't he have had soldiers and guards to protect him? Nurses are not equipped to fight off intruders. Mephibosheth would grow up a cripple because his kingdom did not value the need and role of protectors. David learned from this and ensured that the royal family was always protected during his reign.

Sometimes, we even have to protect kings from themselves. Kings are also mere men, and they make mistakes. Protectors are there to protect the kings from their mistakes. The mistakes of kings are magnified to national proportions. If a king and a gardener make the same mistake, the king will be scrutinized, analyzed, and critiqued by the whole nation, while the gardener only needs to explain to his wife. For this reason, the king will need the help of his protectors to shield him from unnecessary exposure. As pastor and husband, I have made mistakes that could have crippled me. But the men around have helped by taking some of the pressure off me and helped me by carrying the burden. When a king is left exposed and vulnerable to public scrutiny, he will be distracted from his purpose.

Imagine 50,400 angels to watch over one individual!

I have highlighted already that the Scriptures refer to us believers as kings here on earth. This means all believers have a right to a "security detail" that provides protection. Let's look at two profound Scriptures together. The first is from Jesus when He was about to be arrested by the Jews. Peter came to His defense but Jesus stopped him saying, *"Put your sword back in its place! Everyone who uses a sword will be killed by a sword. **Don't you think that I could call on my Father, and he would send me more than twelve legions of angels now?"** (Matthew 26:53).* This passage of Scripture allows us to see that Jesus knew that He had a legal right to be protected by God's angels. We too have this privilege. God promises to protect us. It astonishes me that God spares no expense to see us protected! Jesus said twelve legions of angels were at the ready to protect Him. A legion by definition is a large military unit trained for combat. During the Roman era, a legion consisted of 4,000–6,000 infantry men and about 200–400 cavalry troops. Since Jesus lived in the Roman era, we can assume that He was saying there were at least 50,400 angels at His side ready to protect Him. Fifty thousand, four hundred angels to watch over one man!

Like Jesus, each believer today, has legions of angels watching over his life. It sounds like a bit too much! To God it is not too much—that is how precious we are to Him. What I am saying here is emphasized in the second passage of Scripture I want you to look at. Look at 2 Kings when Elisha's camp was surrounded by the armies of Aram:

> *So the king of Aram **sent out horses, chariots, and an elite force,** and they arrived during the night and surrounded the city. Meanwhile, the attendant to the man of God got up early in the morning and went outside, and there were the **elite forces, surrounding the city, accompanied by horses and chariots!** So Elisha's attendant cried out to him, "Oh no! Master! What will we do!?" Elisha replied, **"Stop being afraid, because there are more with us than with them!"** Then Elisha prayed, asking the LORD, "Please make him able to really see!" And so when the LORD enabled the young man to see, he looked, and there was the mountain, **filled with horses and fiery chariots surrounding Elisha!** (2 Kings 6:14-16).*

God is more than able to protect us. Just like with Jesus and Elisha, God surrounds our lives with His armies. If our earthy countries spend millions of dollars protecting their Presidents, God spends trillions of trillions of dollars on protection per Christian. He treasures us that much.

If God goes to great lengths to see His kings pro-tected on earth, I think it is prudent for us to also protect our kings and leaders in our churches and organizations. Every kingdom needs a protector. Without one, the position of king will have the highest turnover.

Conclusion

The Greatest Kingdom

I hope these twelve principles have helped you. Even though I centered this book on Joseph and Pharaoh, the principles applied are a pattern throughout the Bible. I have tried to show you several examples from the Bible, highlighting these patterns. Where there is a pattern in the Bible, there is a principle to be learned. When you live by these principles you will succeed.

The greatest kingdom ever to exist is God's Kingdom. This Kingdom should be the standard by which we measure our churches and organizations. The Bible encourages us to imitate Christ—our kingdom, too, must imitate the Kingdom of God. If our kingdoms do not resemble the characteristics of the Kingdom of God, my fear is that we are building and managing kingdoms that are carnal in nature and subsequently will eventually fade away. It doesn't matter, how big you think your kingdom is; if it is not a reflection of the Kingdom of God, it will die.

I am all about kingdom building and edifying His Kingdom. I want to influence my generation like Joseph did his. I believe all Christians should have the same aim. We can achieve this by following the Kingdom principles revealed to us by our Lord.

God did not create us to be followers and to conform to the patterns of this world. He wants us to lead, impact and influence. This is what Joseph did—he was a leader who impacted the nation and influenced the region. I am tired of churches and Christians that have no leadership, impact and influence on their communities.

In my church, I always declare that we are Kingdom people, and we have a Kingdom disposition. I pray the same for you.

Made in the USA
Monee, IL
24 August 2022

12387873R00066